First Women in Space

Terry Barber

FAMOUS
FIRSTS
SERIES

First Women in Space is published by
Grass Roots Press, a division of Literacy Services of Canada Ltd.

PHONE 1–888–303–3213
WEBSITE www.literacyservices.com

ACKNOWLEDGEMENTS

We acknowledge the financial support of the Government of Canada through the Book Publishing Industry Development Program (BPIDP) for our publishing activities.

We acknowledge the support of
the Alberta Foundation for the Arts
for our publishing programs.

Editor: Dr. Pat Campbell
Image research: Dr. Pat Campbell
Book design: Lara Minja, Lime Design Inc.
Book layout: Andrée-Ann Thivierge, jellyfish design

Library and Archives Canada Cataloguing in Publication

Barber, Terry, date
        First women in space / Terry Barber.

(Famous Firsts series)
ISBN 978-1-894593-67-0

        1. Women astronauts--Biography. 2. Readers for new literates. I. Title.

PE1126.N43B36437 2007   428.6'2   C2007-902787-3

Printed in Canada.

Contents

These boys want to be the first to spot Sputnik, 1957.

The Space Race

It is 1957. The sky is dark. The little boys look to the sky. "Can you see it?" their grandpa asks. The boys see the light move in the sky. The light blinks. "That's Sputnik," their grandpa says.

Sputnik is the size of a beach ball. It weighs 83.2 kg (183 pounds).

This man checks Sputnik before it goes into space.

The Space Race

Sputnik shocks the world. It is the first space object to circle the Earth. Sputnik is built by the **U.S.S.R.** Sputnik leads to change. It marks the start of the space age. Sputnik starts the space race.

U.S.S.R. stands for the Union of Soviet Socialist Republics.

Sputnik stamp.

The U.S.S.R. sends Yuri Gagarin
into space on April 12, 1961.

The Space Race

On April 12, 1961, the U.S.S.R. puts the first man into space. The U.S. feels uneasy. The U.S. wants to win the space race. The U.S. fears the U.S.S.R. will win. The U.S. sends a man into space 23 days later.

Yuri Gagarin.

A moon walk, 1972.

The Space Race

Today, over 450 people have gone into space. More than 40 of these people have been women. People have died in space. People have lived in space for over a year. They have walked in space. People have walked on the moon.

Neil Armstrong is the first man to walk on the moon.

Valentina Tereshkova, 1963.

Valentina Tereshkova

The first woman to fly into space is from the U.S.S.R. Her name is Valentina Tereshkova. She goes into space on June 16, 1963. She flies **solo.** Valentina circles the Earth in just 89 minutes. She circles the Earth 48 times.

Valentina is born on March 6, 1937.

Valentina sees the Earth.

Valentina Tereshkova

Valentina is in space for three days.
She sees the Earth. It looks so small.
She sees the rivers and oceans. The
rivers look like blue ribbons. She sees
the mountains. She sees large cities.
Valentina takes many pictures.

Crowds welcome Valentina home.
Red Square, Moscow.

Valentina Tereshkova

Valentina's flight makes her very famous. She is a hero in the U.S.S.R. Crowds gather to welcome her home. She gets many honours. Her fame grows. She is a hero to many women in the world.

A U.S.S.R. stamp honours Valentina.

Valentina Tereshkova and her husband,
Andrian Nikolayev, 1965.

Valentina Tereshkova

In 1963, Valentina gets married. Valentina and her husband share a **passion** for flying. The next year, they have a child.

Valentina enters politics in 1966. She retires from politics in 1991.

Sally Ride.

Sally Ride

Years go by. Women do not go into space for 19 years. Then in 1982, the U.S.S.R. sends a second woman into space. A year later, the U.S. sends its first woman into space. Her name is Sally Ride.

Sally Ride is born on May 26, 1951.

In 1978, Sally joins NASA. She wants to be an astronaut.

NASA hires six women in 1978.
(Sally is on the right.)

Sally Ride

Sally grows up in California. She has a goal. She wants to be a scientist. Sally goes to university. She gets her **Ph.D.** People call her Dr. Sally Ride.

NASA stands for the National Aeronautics and Space Administration.

Sally trains by hanging from a parachute.

Sally Ride

NASA thinks Sally is the perfect person to go into space. She is a good athlete. Her body is strong and fit. She has a good mind. Sally is a quick problem solver. Sally has all the "right stuff" to go into space.

Sally Ride and her team.

Sally Ride

NASA also likes Sally because she is a team player. Sally joins a five-person team. They train for a space flight. Each person has a special job. They depend on each other to do their jobs.

Sally trains for five years before her first space flight.

Sally's space ship is called the Challenger.

The Challenger leaves the U.S.

Sally Ride

It is June 18, 1983. The space ship
leaves the U.S. Sally is in space. A long
day ends. Her bed is beside a window.
She can see the Earth. The view takes
her breath away.

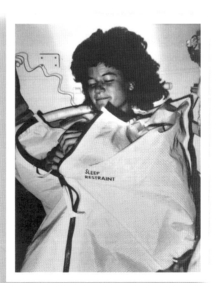

Sally sleeps in
the space ship.

Sally speaks to girls and young women.

Sally Ride

Sally becomes famous after the flight. She uses her fame to promote science. Sally speaks to young women. Sally **inspires** them to study science. Young women follow Sally's footsteps. More women become scientists and astronauts. Sally is a **role model.**

Svetlana Savitskaya is the first
U.S.S.R. woman to walk in space.

First Women to Walk in Space

In 1984, the first woman walks in space. She is from the U.S.S.R. She walks in space for 3 1/2 hours. Later that year, another woman walks in space. She is from the U.S. Slowly, more and more women are becoming astronauts.

Kathryn Sullivan is the first U.S. woman to walk in space.

NASA invites other countries to join its space program.

Roberta Bondar

NASA wants other countries to join its space program. This is a good way for NASA to raise money. Canada joins the space program. In 1983, Canada puts an ad in newspapers. Canada wants to hire six astronauts. Roberta Bondar applies for the job.

Over 4,000 Canadians apply for the job.

Roberta Bondar

Canada needs six people with a good education. They must be fit and strong. And they need to be confident. Over 4,000 people apply for the six jobs. Roberta Bondar is the only woman who makes the **short list**.

A six-year old child applies for the job. So does a 73-year-old housewife.

Roberta's good news is the **icing on the cake.**

Roberta Bondar

It is December 3, 1983. Roberta is at her birthday party. She waits by the phone. At last, the phone rings. She picks it up. Roberta is told that she got the job. Roberta looks at her guests. She says: "I'm in! I'm in!"

Roberta Bondar is Canada's first woman astronaut.

Roberta Bondar

Roberta has the "right stuff," just like Sally Ride. Roberta is a good athlete. She is a quick learner. Hard work does not scare Roberta. Her hard work pays off. In 1992, Roberta flies in space.

Roberta is the only woman on the space flight.

Roberta sits in an art gallery that sells her pictures.

Roberta Bondar

Roberta works at NASA for ten more years. She works as a scientist. In her free time, Roberta writes books. She also takes pictures. Her books include many nature pictures. One of her books is called *Touching the Earth*.

Roberta has written four books.

These women are **trailblazers.**

Trailblazers

Today, a woman going into space is not big news. Women have shown they are equal to men. Women perform just as well as men in space. The first women in space have left a path for others to follow.

Glossary

icing on the cake: an extra benefit to something already good.

inspire: to encourage somebody to do something.

passion: a strong feeling.

Ph.D.: these three letters mean Doctor of Philosophy.

role model: a person whose behaviour is copied by others.

short list: a final list of applicants for a position.

solo: alone.

trailblazer: a person who leads the way.

U.S.S.R.: This nation was formed in 1922 and dissolved in 1991.

Talking About the Book

Why was Sputnik an important moment
in history?

Why do you think the U.S. felt uneasy
when the U.S.S.R. was winning the space race?

What did you learn about Valentina
Tereshkova?

What did you learn about Sally Ride?

What did you learn about Roberta Bondar?

Would you accept an invitation
to go into space? Why or why not?

Picture Credits